D1252463

MIGUEL CAIRO
SECOND BASEMAN

TAMPA BAY
RAYS

FRED McGRIFF
FIRST BASEMAN

TAMPA BAY
RAYS

THE STORY OF THE TAMPA BAY RAYS

Published by Creative Education
P.O. Box 227, Mankato, Minnesota 56002
Creative Education is an imprint of The Creative Company
www.thecreativecompany.us

Design and production by Blue Design
Art direction by Rita Marshall
Printed by Corporate Graphics in the United States of America

Photographs by Getty Images (Kevin C. Cox, Tom DiPace/Sports Illustrated, Elsa, Otto Greule Jr, Nick Laham, Scott Jordan Levy/Time & Life Pictures, G. Newman Lowrance, Brad Mangin/MLB Photos Jim McIsaac, J. Meric, Peter Muhly/AFP, Tom Pigeon/Allsport, Anne Rippy, Jim Rogash, Robert Rogers/MLB Photos, David Seelig/Allsport, Ron Vesely/MLB Photos, John Williamson/MLB Photos)

Library of Congress Cataloging-in-Publication Data

LeBoutillier, Nate.
The story of the Tampa Bay Rays / by Nate LeBoutillier.
p. cm. — (Baseball: the great American game)
Includes index.
Summary: The history of the Tampa Bay Rays professional baseball team from its inaugural 1998 season to today, spotlighting the team's greatest players and most memorable moments.
ISBN 978-1-60818-057-8
1. Tampa Bay Rays (Baseball team)—History—Juvenile literature. I. Title. II. Series.

GV875.T26L43 2011
796.357'640975965—dc22   2010025477

CPSIA: 110310 PO1381

First Edition
9 8 7 6 5 4 3 2 1

Page 3: Outfielder Delmon Young
Page 4: Third baseman Evan Longoria

BASEBALL: THE GREAT AMERICAN GAME

THE STORY OF THE TAMPA BAY RAYS

Nate LeBoutillier

CREATIVE EDUCATION

CONTENTS

CHAPTERS

A Devilish Debut 6

Treading Water 15

Lou Leads the Way 22

The Kazmir Years 29

Rays Redemption 34

AROUND THE HORN

Just Visiting 12

Tampa Bay's Home Turf 20

A Game with Two Ends 24

Tampa Bay Turns a Triple 31

Change for the Better 38

The Skipper's Ride 43

ALL-TIME RAYS

P — Scott Kazmir 8

C — Toby Hall 13

1B — Fred McGriff 14

2B — Miguel Cairo 18

3B — Evan Longoria 23

SS — Julio Lugo 28

LF — Carl Crawford 30

CF — Randy Winn 35

RF — Aubrey Huff 39

M — Joe Maddon 40

Index 48

A DEVILISH DEBUT

Archaeologists believe that humans known as Paleo-Indians existed in Florida 12,000 to 14,000 years ago and that a tribe known as the Manasota lived in the Tampa Bay area as far back as 4000 B.C. It's not hard to see why early peoples might have chosen to inhabit this place, as it features abundant sea, sun, and sand, as well as warm temperatures year round. Today, when people speak of the "Tampa Bay area," they are usually referring most specifically to the two large, neighboring cities of Tampa and St. Petersburg.

In 1998, a professional baseball team also made itself at home next to this bay. It was then, after the area had already spent decades playing host to big-league baseball teams holding spring training in south Florida, that Tampa Bay first fielded a Major League Baseball team of its own. Thanks to a public "name-the-team" contest, the new American League (AL) club took the field as the "Devil Rays." A common sight in the Bay waters, devil rays (also called manta rays) are odd-looking marine creatures that get their name from unique fins near their heads that resemble devils' horns.

Tampa (pictured) and neighboring St. Petersburg lend themselves to indoor baseball, as the cities feature hot, humid, and often stormy summers.

PITCHER · SCOTT KAZMIR

After a legendary high school career (in which he once threw no-hitters in four consecutive outings) Scott Kazmir bypassed college when he was drafted by the New York Mets in 2002. Two seasons later, Tampa Bay traded away the best pitcher it had had in its short history, Victor Zambrano, for Kazmir, who was showing promise in the minors. By season's end, Kazmir was in the big leagues, blowing hitters away with his exploding fastball. In 2007, the staff ace led the AL in strikeouts with 239, and in 2008, he helped propel the Rays to their first playoff appearance.

STATS

Rays seasons: 2004–09

Height: 6 feet

Weight: 180

- 993 career strikeouts

- 66–61 career record

- 4.14 career ERA

- 2-time All-Star

SCOTT KAZMIR
PITCHER

TAMPA BAY
RAYS

The Tampa Bay franchise was truly born in 1995, when Major League Baseball announced that the area would receive a new expansion franchise. In July 1995, former Atlanta Braves scout and executive Chuck LaMar was named the Devil Rays' general manager, and Larry Rothschild, a respected major-league pitching coach who had never before managed a game, was named the team's skipper. The Devil Rays made their first major-league trade on November 11, 1997, acquiring lanky outfielder Mike Kelly from the Cincinnati Reds. "I was thrilled," said Kelly, "because I knew it meant I was getting an opportunity to play, and that's what it's all about."

A week later, the Devil Rays used their first pick in a special expansion draft to select pitcher Tony Saunders, who had been a member of the World Series-winning Florida Marlins the year before. By the time the draft concluded, the Rays had selected 35 players, including quick center fielder Quinton McCracken and veteran catcher Mike Difelice. After the draft, Tampa Bay continued to add talent via trades and free-agent signings, obtaining hard-hitting first baseman and Tampa native Fred "Crime Dog" McGriff, shortstop Kevin Stocker, and pitchers Roberto Hernandez and Wilson Alvarez. "It's been the most exciting week I can remember," said LaMar, "to sit down with the 28 other general managers for the first time and talk trades."

The Devil Rays debuted before a sold-out crowd in St. Petersburg's Tropicana Field on March 31, 1998. Playing against the Detroit Tigers, the Devil Rays lost 11–6 but returned the next day to best Detroit with hits in eight of nine innings. With Cuban pitcher Rolando Arrojo in control on the mound and McGriff driving in four runs, the Devil Rays thrilled their fans with a retributive 11–8 victory.

By mid-April, the Devil Rays were the first expansion team ever to be 4 games over .500 in its inaugural season with a 10–6 record. Despite the promising start and solid contributions from Arrojo, McCracken, McGriff, and youngsters such as second baseman Miguel Cairo and rangy outfielder Randy Winn, the Devil Rays fell into last place in the AL Eastern Division and stayed there, finishing the season 63–99.

Tampa Bay started its second year a respectable 22–20. Much of that season's excitement came from veteran players achieving career milestones in Devil Rays uniforms. Strapping outfielder Jose Canseco, who had signed

WADE BOGGS

Like many baseball players, Wade Boggs had his superstitions. He ate the same meal (chicken) before every game, and he took exactly 100 ground balls during practice. After his playing career, he took up residence in Tampa.

JUST VISITING

Although Tampa Bay didn't claim its own Major League Baseball team until 1998, professional baseball had been a part of the area since the early 1900s. Starting in 1913, the Chicago Cubs made Tampa their home for spring training baseball, since the location let them hold preseason practices in much more comfortable temperatures than Illinois offered. The next year, the St. Louis Browns followed suit in neighboring St. Petersburg, and soon the Grapefruit League—a five-week series of preseason games between teams training in Florida—was born. Today, almost all major-league teams hold their spring training in Florida or Arizona.

Tampa Bay's appeal as a permanent baseball market was not lost on the league; in the 1980s, teams such as the Minnesota Twins, Oakland Athletics, Chicago White Sox, Texas Rangers, Seattle Mariners, and San Francisco Giants all flirted with the prospect of moving to Tampa Bay as they faced difficulties in their own various home cities. Yet despite such talk, the Tampa Bay area remained without a major-league team by the end of the 1980s. In 1986, Bay area officials constructed a major-league-capacity, domed stadium (originally named the Florida Suncoast Dome) in order to attract a baseball franchise, and finally, in 1998, the Devil Rays arrived.

CATCHER · TOBY HALL

Toby Hall split time between the Devil Rays' big-league roster and minor-league teams between 2000 and 2002 before he was finally named full-time catcher for Tampa Bay in 2003. On August 20 of that season, he homered in the top of the ninth inning off Seattle Mariners pitcher Shigetoshi Hasegawa to give Rays manager Lou Piniella a 60th birthday present: a 3–2 win. The burly catcher, who often wore a red beard and was known for his strong arm, threw out 43 percent of would-be base stealers in 2003 and drove in a career-high 60 runs in 2004.

TOBY HALL
CATCHER

TAMPA BAY
RAYS

STATS

Rays seasons: 2000–06

Height: 6-foot-2

Weight: 230

- .262 career BA

- 46 career HR

- 269 career RBI

- .989 fielding percentage

FIRST BASEMAN · FRED McGRIFF

Tampa Bay acquired offensive powerhouse Fred "Crime Dog" McGriff from the Atlanta Braves in its inaugural season. A feared fastball hitter with a smooth swing, the lanky first baseman delivered 32 homers for the Devil Rays during the 1999 season, and in 2000, he slugged 27 more, including the 400th of his career. In a 2000 game against the Baltimore Orioles, the Tampa native hit a home run in his 37th different ballpark. He signed with the Rays again in 2004, hoping to slug 9 homers and reach the prestigious 500 mark, but he retired in July after hitting only 2.

STATS

Rays seasons: 1998–2001, 2004

Height: 6-foot-3

Weight: 215

- 5-time All-Star

- 2-time league leader in HR (once in AL, once in NL)

- 1994 All-Star Game MVP

- 493 career HR

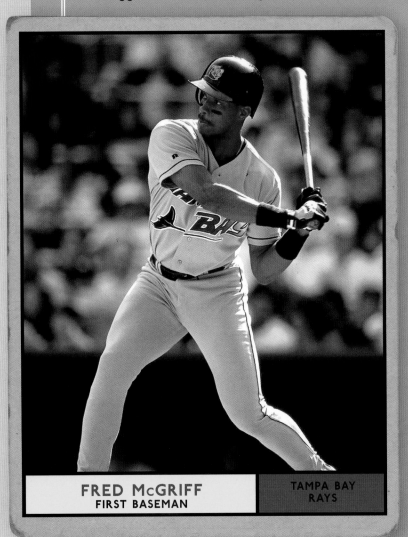

FRED McGRIFF
FIRST BASEMAN

TAMPA BAY
RAYS

with Tampa Bay before the start of the season, blasted his 400th career home run on April 14. Devil Rays fans also went wild on August 7 when third baseman Wade Boggs, a Tampa native, became the first player in the history of baseball to pop a home run for his 3,000th career hit.

Such individual heroics were not enough to keep the team afloat, however, as the Devil Rays were plagued by injuries. As the losses mounted, fan support dwindled. Average attendance at Tropicana Field dropped below 20,000 a game, even though the team showed improvement by going 69–93.

TREADING WATER

n an effort to make its 2000 team more competitive, Tampa Bay fished for some affordable big-name players in the off-season. The Devil Rays thought they caught their limit when they netted two heavy hitters: slugging third baseman Vinny Castilla and All-Star outfielder Greg Vaughn, both of whom came over from National League teams. "I'm not a savior by any means," said Vaughn, who had slammed 45

home runs and posted 118 runs batted in (RBI) for the Reds the year before. "I'm just a small piece of the puzzle. I think we have a pretty good shot at doing some things."

With the additions, Tampa Bay's lineup suddenly consisted of powerhouse hitters McGriff, Canseco, Vaughn, and Castilla. Hopes quickly evaporated, however, when instead of blasting balls out of the park, three of the four sluggers suffered slumps and injuries. Only McGriff finished the 2000 season healthy, putting up 106 RBI. In September, the team limped through a 2–16 stretch despite some solid pitching by hurlers Albie Lopez, Bryan Rekar, and Esteban Yan. The Devil Rays ended the season in last place in the AL East once again with a 69–92 mark.

Hoping to shake loose of their struggling ways, team management fired Larry Rothschild in April 2001 and replaced him with Devil Rays bench coach Hal McRae, who was known for his intense personality. McRae stated a litany of simple goals for his club. "We're going to catch it, hit it, and throw it better," he said. "Our players will be on time, play hard, play to win, and play unselfish baseball."

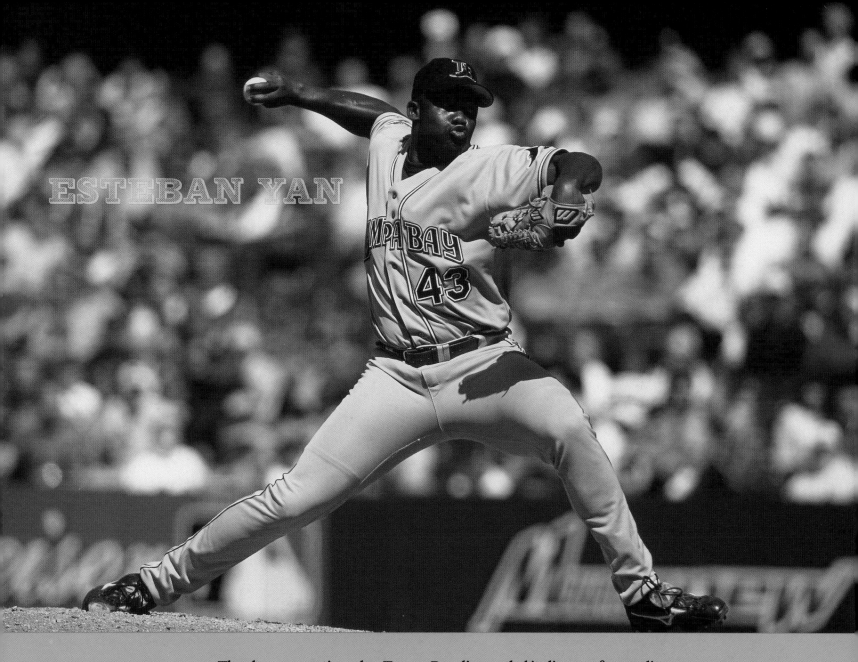

ESTEBAN YAN

The changes continued as Tampa Bay dismantled its lineup of struggling heavy hitters, releasing Castilla and trading McGriff to the Chicago Cubs for young infielder Jason Smith. Vaughn, the only one of the big boppers who remained, batted a miserable .233 with just 24 homers in 2001 as the team racked up a whopping 100 losses, finishing in last place again. As if to rub salt in the wound, Tampa Bay players and fans then had to look on as the

SECOND BASEMAN · MIGUEL CAIRO

For the first three years of the Devil Rays' existence, Venezuelan Miguel Cairo manned second base for the young franchise. In 1999, the keen-eyed Cairo ranked as the AL's eighth-most difficult strikeout target, getting "K'd" only once every 11 plate appearances on average and posting a .295 batting average with a 12-game hitting streak. Renowned for his accurate throws and wide-ranging fielding ability, he posted the league's third-highest fielding percentage in 2000. Cairo also displayed impressive speed on the base paths, swiping a team-record 28 bases that same season, including 2 in a single inning against the Seattle Mariners.

MIGUEL CAIRO
SECOND BASEMAN

TAMPA BAY
RAYS

STATS

Rays seasons: 1998–2000

Height: 6-foot-1

Weight: 200

- .984 career fielding percentage

- .294 career playoff BA

- 348 career RBI

- 132 career stolen bases

Arizona Diamondbacks—a team born the same year as the Devil Rays—moved onward and upward to win the World Series that season.

In 2002, the Devil Rays started with a bang, winning three straight games against the Tigers. But dark clouds returned as Tampa Bay surrendered three consecutive games to the New York Yankees and soon thereafter suffered its first no-hitter, losing 10–0 at the hands of Red Sox hurler Derek Lowe at Boston's Fenway Park. The team endured its longest losing streak (15 games) yet before Winn hit a three-run, walk-off home run on May 11 against the Baltimore Orioles to give the Rays a 6–4 victory. "This one was big because it gets the monkey off our back," Winn said. "We were getting a lot of attention for something negative."

Fans cheered some encouraging individual performances, such as the play of speedy young outfielder Carl Crawford and the hitting of third baseman Aubrey Huff, who ended the year with 23 home runs and a .313 batting average. But the Devil Rays attracted fewer than a million people to home games all season and finished in last place again in the AL East with an embarrassing mark of 55–106.

TAMPA BAY'S HOME TURF

When a pro baseball team failed to take up residence at St. Petersburg's Florida Suncoast Dome, the National Hockey League's Tampa Bay Lightning franchise moved into the empty stadium in 1993 and changed the venue's name to the Thunderdome. Three years later, the Lightning built a new arena, the Ice Palace, and the owners of the Thunderdome reconverted it to a ballfield to accommodate the expansion Devil Rays. Renamed Tropicana Field (after a deal with the juice-making sponsor paid $13 million to the city of St. Petersburg), the revamped park featured all-dirt base paths and FieldTurf, a natural-looking synthetic grass. An eight-story-high mosaic containing 1.8 million colored tiles depicting the sun, sea, and beach welcomed guests, who might visit a café located directly behind the Rays' bullpen in the right-field corner; a spa at "The Beach," a concourse on the second level behind left field complete with palm trees and employees wearing Hawaiian shirts; or a climbing wall on the Center Field Street concourse. The world's second-largest cable-supported domed roof, built to withstand hurricane gales of up to 115 miles per hour, was lit a luminous orange at night when the Devil Rays won a home game.

LOU LEADS THE WAY

Before the 2003 season, the Devil Rays hired a new dugout leader: Tampa native Lou Piniella, one of the most successful managers of the previous decade. Cincinnati had won the 1990 World Series under Piniella, and in a subsequent 10-year managerial reign with the Seattle Mariners, Piniella's team went 840–711 and reached the AL Championship Series (ALCS) in 1995, 2000, and 2001. The fiery Piniella had also led the Mariners to an AL-record 116 wins in 2001 and captured league Manager of the Year honors. "I look forward to the challenge, and it's going to be fun," Piniella said upon his hiring. "Managing a baseball team for me is a special privilege, and when you can do it in your hometown, it's even nicer."

After putting Piniella at the helm, the Devil Rays signed some veteran players, including outfielder Al Martin, utility infielder Terry Shumpert, and southpaw pitcher Mike Venafro. Tampa Bay also added two talented rookies to the roster: pitcher Seth McClung and outfielder Rocco Baldelli. McClung added some smoke to

LOU PINIELLA

THIRD BASEMAN · EVAN LONGORIA

After a meteoric rise through the Tampa Bay minor-league system that started in 2006, Evan Longoria was ready to bring his long ball to the major leagues. The Rays couldn't resist promoting Longoria up from the minors only 2 weeks into the 2008 season, whereupon he started launching homers and didn't stop, finishing with 27 in just 122 games as a rookie.

But Longoria truly introduced himself to the sports world in the playoffs, slamming a total of six homers against the Chicago White Sox and the Boston Red Sox. In 2009, Longoria completed his transformation into an all-around superstar by winning the Gold Glove award for his stellar defense.

EVAN LONGORIA
THIRD BASEMAN

TAMPA BAY
RAYS

STATS

Rays seasons: 2008–present

Height: 6-foot-2

Weight: 210

- 2008 AL Rookie of the Year

- 82 career home runs

- 302 career RBI

- 3-time All-Star

FRED McGRIFF

A GAME WITH TWO ENDS

The Devil Rays were ahead 4–3 with two outs in the bottom of the ninth inning on May 31, 2000, when Baltimore Orioles outfielder B. J. Surhoff hit a grounder to Tampa Bay shortstop Felix Martinez. Martinez fired a one-hopper to Fred McGriff at first, first base umpire Brian Runge called Surhoff out, and the Rays started to congratulate one another. But Orioles manager Mike Hargrove and first base coach Eddie Murray argued Runge's call, pointing to an off-the-bag footprint left by McGriff. Nine minutes later, umpire crew chief John Shulock overruled Runge's call, and both teams were called back onto the Tropicana Field to finish the game—a decision that steamed Devil Rays manager Larry Rothschild. "I don't understand it," Rothschild said. "Yeah, get the call right. But don't let us get off the field and the whole thing. Do you watch a replay after the game and decide you made a bad call so let's go replay it tomorrow?" When the game resumed, Orioles center fielder Charles Johnson hit a single to right field, advancing Surhoff to third. Outfielder Brady Anderson then drew a full count before striking out on a Roberto Hernandez fastball, and the Rays won the one-of-a-kind game (again), 4–3.

the pitching staff, slinging his 97-mile-per-hour fastball to catcher Toby Hall, while the 21-year-old Baldelli's hustle and strong hitting earned him a starting role in center field.

A dramatic, come-from-behind win by the revamped Devil Rays in their 2003 season opener against the Red Sox seemed to trigger a number of dynamic individual performances. Leading the charge was Baldelli, who won AL Rookie of the Month honors in April by going .364 at the plate. Outfielder Ben Grieve made the Devil Rays faithful proud by winning a home run derby held prior to baseball's annual Hall of Fame Game at Cooperstown, New York, in June. And Crawford tore up the base paths, sprinting to the AL stolen base crown with 55 thefts.

Between July 3 and August 19, the Devil Rays enjoyed some of the hottest hitting and finest pitching in franchise history. Huff bashed 7 home runs with 27 RBI during the stretch, while first baseman Travis Lee and lanky shortstop Julio Lugo also knocked the ball around. On the mound, Victor Zambrano and Rob Bell hurled their way to a combined 5–1 mark. Even though the team ended up winning seven games fewer than Piniella's stated preseason goal of 70 (and with its worst home

RAYS

[25]

attendance yet, an average of just 13,070 fans a game), the Rays avoided the dreaded century mark in losses, finishing the 2003 season 63–99.

Hosted by fans in Tokyo, Japan, the Devil Rays won their first game of the 2004 season against the Yankees. Then, in typical Tampa Bay fashion, they lost the next day and 28 of the following 38 games. But things then began to turn around. In June, the club won a whopping 20 games, including a franchise-record 12 in a row, thanks largely to the hot bats of Crawford, Lugo, switch-hitting outfielder Jose Cruz Jr., and first baseman Tino Martinez, who had helped the Yankees win four World Series in the late '90s. But then, just as soon as the Rays attained the .500 mark in July—a first for the team—the Yankees put them in their place with a four-game sweep.

The Rays then reverted to their old ways, losing 12 games in a row in September. Still, as bumpy as the road was, Tampa Bay avoided a last-place finish in the AL East for the first time and compiled its best record yet, 70–91. "We've gone from 55 to 70 wins in 2 years," Piniella said after the season. "What we need to do is not take a step back. We need to keep it going and set a standard for the future."

Rocco Baldelli's speed made him a rookie standout, as he ranked second among all 2003 Devil Rays players in both runs (89) and steals (27).

ROCCO BALDELLI

SHORTSTOP · JULIO LUGO

Dominican-born Julio Lugo, who moved to New York City when he was 12, took over as the Devil Rays' shortstop in May 2003. In 2004, he showed dramatic improvement as a hitter, driving in a career-best 75 runs and leading the Rays in batting with runners in scoring position. He was a versatile hitter, equally adept at driving the ball into outfield gaps, dropping bunts for infield singles, or slapping the ball through the infield on hit-and-runs. In July 2005, he set a team record for hits in a month with 40. Lugo's speed and aggression also made him a valuable base thief.

JULIO LUGO
SHORTSTOP

TAMPA BAY
RAYS

STATS

Rays seasons: 2003–06

Height: 6-foot-1

Weight: 175

- **.270 career BA**

- **1,273 career hits**

- **472 career RBI**

- **198 career stolen bases**

RAYS

[28]

THE KAZMIR YEARS

I t seemed for a while that a big step back was inevitable as the Devil Rays' 2005 season opened miserably; halfway through the season, the team lugged a pitiful 28–61 record. But after July, the Rays began to find their groove. Lugo produced a .295 hitting average that was tops among all major-league shortstops, Crawford scored a team-leading 101 runs, and third baseman Jorge Cantu homered 28 times and drove in 117 runs. Behind these efforts, the Devil Rays went 39–34 after the midseason All-Star break to finish 67–95.

Tampa Bay regressed to a disappointing 61–101 in 2006, but a crew of young players with potential offered hope that better days were ahead. Crawford ran wild with 58 stolen bases, and young left-handed pitcher Scott Kazmir emerged as an All-Star by posting 10 wins before being shelved by injury late in the year. Tampa Bay finished the year pointing in the wrong direction, losing 16 of its last 20 games.

Even though it wasn't obvious yet, the Devil Rays' fortunes were preparing to turn. Before the start of the 2006 season, the club had

LEFT FIELDER · CARL CRAWFORD

Even though he played little organized baseball before entering high school, Carl Crawford was named a Second-Team All-American by *Baseball America* magazine in his senior year in 1999, and he turned down college athletic scholarships for basketball and football to play baseball. He was drafted by Tampa Bay, and after 3 years in the minors, the speedy 20-year-old was called up to the "big show" in the middle of the 2002 season. By season's end, he had earned Tampa Bay's Most Outstanding Rookie honors, and in 2003 and 2004, he stole 114 combined bases, leading the AL in thefts each season.

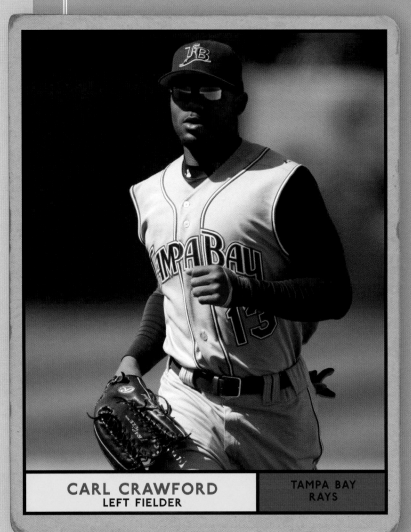

CARL CRAWFORD
LEFT FIELDER

TAMPA BAY
RAYS

STATS

Rays seasons: 2002–2010

Height: 6-foot-2

Weight: 220

- 4-time All-Star

- 4-time AL stolen bases leader

- 4-time AL triples leader

- 2009 All-Star Game MVP

DEWON BRAZELTON

TAMPA BAY TURNS A TRIPLE

A triple play is one of baseball's rarest and most memorable plays. The Devil Rays turned the first in franchise history on September 13, 2002, in the fifth inning against the Blue Jays at Toronto's SkyDome. Tampa Bay rookie pitcher Dewon Brazelton, who had climbed to the major leagues from humble beginnings in Tullahoma, Tennessee, stood on the mound in his major-league debut. Blue Jays shortstop Chris Woodward ripped a single, then second baseman Dave Berg was beaned by a wild Brazelton pitch. Next up was catcher Ken Huckaby, who smacked a line drive at Devil Rays second baseman Andy Sheets. Sheets caught it for the first out, tossed it to shortstop Chris Gomez (who was covering second base) for the second out, and Gomez turned and fired the ball to first baseman Aubrey Huff, who tagged the bag for the third out before Berg, who had jumped out to a lead, could get back. Prior to that game, the most recent triple play turned behind a pitcher throwing his first major-league game occurred on August 31, 1919, with St. Louis Browns pitcher Rolla Mapel on the mound against the Detroit Tigers. Despite the rare triple putout, the Devil Rays lost the game, 5–2.

SCOTT KAZMIR

made a switch at the managerial position, parting ways with Piniella and hiring little-known Joe Maddon, a former bench coach for the Los Angeles Angels of Anaheim. Maddon came with curious credentials. He had helped coach the Angels to a World Series title in 2002, but he'd never played in the major leagues. He wore professorial glasses and had a college degree in economics. Although some fans questioned the hire, Maddon was confident he knew how to improve the team. "I believe the biggest thing we have to do around here is we need to change the culture and the way we interact, and our game plan and our concept," he said after the 2006 season. "That's still probably number one. Before we're ever going to win, we have to get that stuff in order."

The 2007 season was another learning year, as the Rays finished 66–96 and wound up in the basement of the AL East again. Still, good things were happening that didn't necessarily show up in the final score. Kazmir complemented his lively fastball with a devastating changeup, often leaving opposing batters whiffing at air. In fact, the lefty rang up 239 strikeouts, best in the

At 180 pounds, Scott Kazmir was one of baseball's smaller star pitchers, yet his fastball was known to approach 100 miles per hour.

AL, and he put a 13–9 record next to the 12–8 mark of fellow Devil Rays hurler James Shields. At the plate, Tampa Bay got a boost in the form of veteran Carlos Peña, who appeared seemingly out of nowhere to win the first base job in spring training and smack a team-record 46 homers during the season.

RAYS REDEMPTION

nd then, not a season too soon, came the turnaround of 2008. Right out of the gate, the Rays—who had dropped the "Devil" from their name—served notice to AL East powers Boston and New York that they would be a team to be reckoned with. They caught fire in May and never looked back, going from worst to first in the division and notching an incredible 97–65 mark. This seemingly miraculous improvement was sparked in part by such key additions as rangy shortstop Jason Bartlett, electric pitcher Matt Garza, and veteran closer Troy Percival. Rookie third baseman Evan Longoria and speedy outfielder B. J. Upton also burst onto the scene as fast-rising stars.

CENTER FIELDER · RANDY WINN

A versatile athlete, Randy Winn played college basketball at Santa Clara University before the Florida Marlins selected him in the third round of the 1995 amateur draft. Winn debuted with the expansion Devil Rays as the team's center fielder in 1998. He sometimes had trouble tracking fly balls, but his fast feet enabled him to recover and often make astounding defensive plays. Although a quiet, private person off the field who preferred to avoid interviews, Winn spoke volumes with his bat as he ripped pitches down the third-base line and into outfield gaps for frequent doubles and triples.

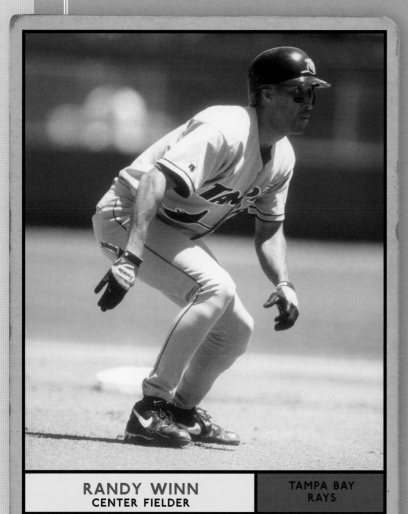

RANDY WINN
CENTER FIELDER

TAMPA BAY
RAYS

STATS

Rays seasons: 1998–2002

Height: 6-foot-2

Weight: 195

• 2002 All-Star

• .284 career batting average

• 662 career RBI

• 215 career stolen bases

The Rays stayed hot in the playoffs, dispatching the Chicago White Sox three games to one in the AL Division Series (ALDS), then winning a thrilling ALCS over the Red Sox, four games to three. In Game 7, designated hitter Willy Aybar hit a double and a homer, and Garza threw a masterful seven innings of two-hit ball to lead the Rays to an unforgettable 3–1 victory. "I didn't know if today was my last start of the year or what," said Garza, "so I just went out there and emptied my tank and said, 'Hey, here goes, we'll see what happens.'" In what surely seemed a dream to longtime Tampa Bay fans, the new-look and new-name Rays were suddenly World Series-bound.

The Rays' World Series opponent was the Philadelphia Phillies. The Phillies eked out a 3–2 win in Game 1 in Tampa before the Rays battled back behind a strong pitching effort from Shields to win Game 2 by a 4–2 score. Unfortunately for Rays fans, that's where the magical ride ended, as the Phillies took the next three games in succession to capture the World Series crown. Still, the defeat did nothing to stifle the sudden swell of pride in Tampa Bay. "My favorite moment from this season has been seeing the faces," Maddon said. "Whether it's our players, the

Matt Garza played for the Minnesota Twins before joining Tampa Bay, rising from the lowest level of the minor leagues to the big leagues in a single season (2006). In 2008, he led all AL pitchers in shutouts, throwing two.

CHANGE FOR THE BETTER

After Tampa Bay suffered its 10th consecutive losing season in 2007, and as fan attendance levels plummeted to new lows, the franchise committed itself to taking a new direction. The team's management started by changing the club's name, slightly, from the Devil Rays to the Rays, although other, more radical, changes in name—such as the Waves, Dukes, Stars, or Cannons—were considered. The team also redesigned its uniforms, dropping green and black as its primary team colors and going with navy, light blue, and gold instead. "We were tied to the past, and the past wasn't necessarily something we wanted to be known for," said team owner Stuart Sternberg. "Nobody's running from it or hiding from it, and we're proud of certain aspects of it, but this is something the organization was able to really put their arms around. I hope and expect the fans who come out will see it as a new beginning." A new beginning it was, and a successful one at that—though the club's maturing players and new coaching staff certainly played a bigger role than names or colors—as the 2008 Rays went out and streaked to the playoffs for the first time in team history.

RIGHT FIELDER · AUBREY HUFF

Good mechanics, enough bat speed to catch up to the fastest fastball, and a knack for spotting breaking balls and changeup pitches made Aubrey Huff one of the steadiest hitters in Devil Rays history. His sweet swing produced 926 hits and 487 RBI for Tampa Bay, and he became the first player in team history to hit 100 home runs. Huff—who bore an uncanny resemblance to television host Conan O'Brien—was a more than capable performer in the field as well, spending time not only in right field but in left field, at third base, and at first.

STATS

Rays seasons: 2000–06

Height: 6-foot-4

Weight: 230

- **229 career HR**
- **838 career RBI**
- **.283 career BA**
- **84 extra-base hits in 2003**

AUBREY HUFF
RIGHT FIELDER

TAMPA BAY
RAYS

MANAGER · JOE MADDON

Big-league benches are littered with managers and coaches who once played the game at the major-league level themselves. Not so for Tampa Bay's Joe Maddon, a one-time catcher who never made it out of the minors. But that didn't matter when Maddon presided over the first winning Tampa Bay team in franchise history in 2008 and then took the Rays all the way to the World Series. "He's very calm, quiet, and trusting," said Rays pitcher James Shields. "Sometimes you have a manager who yells at you every night, but he doesn't do that. He'll sit you down and talk to you and teach you."

STATS

Rays seasons as manager: 2006–present

Managerial record: 431–430

AL pennant: 2008

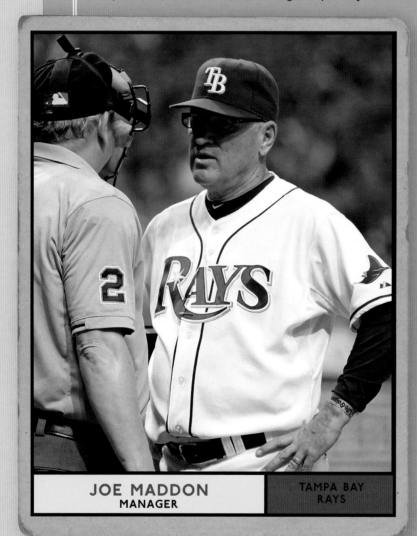

JOE MADDON
MANAGER

TAMPA BAY
RAYS

guys who work in our clubhouse, the training staff, the guys upstairs, the front office people, the guys who've been here so many years, to see the looks on their faces right now and how happy they are that all the negativity has been laid to rest. We have a bright future ahead of us."

The 2009 Rays came back hungry but faltered in the season's first month, going 9–14. Soon, though, the solid play of some young stars got the team back on track. Longoria and Peña started cranking homers with regularity, and in one game, Crawford tied the major-league record for stolen bases in a single game with six. The Rays heated up in June and pushed their record to 44–35 before hitting a rough patch that ultimately derailed their bid to win back-to-back AL East titles.

Rays fans endured another disappointment when, in August, team management traded Kazmir to the Angels. The move did not sit well with many players and fans, partly because of the pitcher's popularity, and partly because Tampa Bay was only 5 games out in the race for a Wild Card berth into the playoffs. But the small-market Rays decided that Kazmir's large salary would be better spent on several up-and-coming pitchers such as Andy Sonnanstine, Wade Davis, and David

Price. "I was surprised," said Kazmir, the franchise's career leader in wins, strikeouts, earned run average (ERA), and games started. "I just want to say thanks to the organization for all the years I've been here— all the support they've given me."

Despite the trade, the Rays capped the season with their second straight winning mark (84–78), though they fell short of the Wild Card spot. In the off-season, Tampa Bay continued to load up on new talent, obtaining hard-hitting catcher Kelly Shoppach and veteran closer Rafael Soriano in separate trades. "We're arriving at the point where we are developing the Rays' way of doing things," said Maddon as the 2010 season approached. "You can see a level of comfort in regard to the interaction among everybody. I can see what we're doing right now sustaining itself for many years to come."

The Rays made a strong surge again in 2010, fending off the Yankees to win the AL East with a 96–66 mark and returning to the playoffs, this time with home-field advantage. Unfortunately, the club's postseason lasted only one series this time, as Tampa Bay slumped at the plate and fell to the Texas Rangers. The ALDS made baseball history as the first playoff series ever in which the road team won every game.

THE SKIPPER'S RIDE

As a bench coach for the Anaheim Angels from 1996 to 2005, Joe Maddon was known for more than just his baseball wisdom and easygoing way with players. He was also known for his bicycle. Most road trips, Maddon would take apart his bike from top to bottom so it would fit on the team plane, and then he would put it back together again so he could take it on long rides that totaled upwards of 100 miles per week. Once he became the Rays' manager in 2006 and was armed with the heftier salary that such a position commands, he usually saved himself the packing and just rented a bike to ride when the Rays visited opposing teams' cities. "In Boston, I ride up and down the Charles and end up at Boston College," explained the skipper, who made a point of exploring as much as he could. "Toronto has a great path along the lake. In Chicago, I go downtown past Comiskey Park, and the only time I've been to Wrigley Field was on my bicycle. In San Francisco, I rode over the Golden Gate Bridge and stopped in the middle, checking out Alcatraz. That was a bit religious there, very cool."

CARLOS PEÑA

Carlos Peña perfected his power stroke in 2007. Over the next 4 seasons, he averaged 36 home runs and 101 RBI per year for the fast-rising Rays.

DAVID PRICE

Thanks in part to the superb hurling of David Price (opposite) and the defense of
second baseman Ben Zobrist (below), the 2010 Rays posted the best record in the AL.

Tampa Bay baseball fans have had to be a patient lot. After waiting
nearly a century for their own major-league team, they had to endure a
decade of losing before experiencing the bliss of a World Series. As the
Tampa Bay faithful continue to throw their support behind their young,
newly named, and suddenly powerful Rays, fans in south Florida may
very well see a world champion soon rise up by the bay.

BEN ZOBRIST

INDEX

AL pennant 40

Alvarez, Wilson 10

Arrojo, Rolando 10

Aybar, Willy 36

Baldelli, Rocco 22, 25

Bartlett, Jason 34

Bell, Robb 25

Boggs, Wade 15

Brazelton, Dewon 31

Cairo, Miguel 10, 18

Canseco, Jose 10, 15, 16

Cantu, Jorge 29

Castilla, Vinny 15, 16, 17

Crawford, Carl 19, 25, 26, 29, 30, 41

Cruz, Jose Jr. 26

Davis, Wade 41

Difelice, Mike 9

division championship 42

Florida spring training 6, 12

    Grapefruit League 12

Florida Suncoast Dome 12, 20

Garza, Matt 34, 36

Gold Glove award 23

Gomez, Chris 31

Grieve, Ben 25

Hall, Toby 13, 25

Hernandez, Roberto 10, 24

Huff, Aubrey 19, 25, 31, 39

Kazmir, Scott 8, 29, 33–34, 41, 42

Kelly, Mike 9

LaMar, Chuck 9, 10

Lee, Travis 25

Longoria, Evan 23, 34, 41

Lopez, Albie 16

Lugo, Julio 25, 26, 28, 29

Maddon, Joe 33, 36, 40, 41, 42, 43

major-league records 41

Martin, Al 22

Martinez, Felix 24

Martinez, Tino 26

McClung, Seth 22, 25

McCracken, Quinton 9, 10

McGriff, Fred 9, 10, 14, 16, 17, 24

McRae, Hal 16

MVP award 14, 30

Peña, Carlos 34, 41

Percival, Troy 34

Piniella, Lou 13, 22, 25, 26, 33

playoffs 8, 23, 36, 38, 42

    AL Championship Series 36

    AL Division Series 36, 42

Price, David 41–42

Rekar, Bryan 16

Rookie of the Year award 23

Rothschild, Larry 9, 16, 24

Saunders, Tony 9

Sheets, Andy 31

Shields, James 34, 36, 40

Shoppach, Kelly 42

Shumpert, Terry 22

Smith, Jason 17

Sonnanstine, Andy 41

Soriano, Rafael 42

Sternberg, Stuart 38

Stocker, Kevin 9

team name 6, 34, 38

team records 18, 26, 28, 34

Tropicana Field 10, 12, 15, 20, 24

Upton, B. J. 34

Vaughn, Greg 15–16, 17

Venafro, Mike 22

Winn, Randy 10, 19, 35

World Series 36, 40, 47

Yan, Esteban 16

Zambrano, Victor 8, 25